let's play

a game with Charlie

Thank you to the coaches and SMAC® team members for believing in this project and to my friends and family. A special thanks to contributors Robyn, Dean, Mel, Trevor and Charlie Figallo OSJ OAM.

To my family Renee, Tanisha, Lachlan, Rachel, Baden and Riley, thank you for being there for me.

Let's Play a game with Charlie
ISBN 978-0-6481963-5-8
Copyright © 2022 John Connelly. All rights reserved.
Design by John Connelly
Illustrations by Dean Lahn, John Connelly and Robyn Souphandavong
Editing by Melissa Riley
First Published in Australia 2022 by SMAC® The Art of Change™

let's play

a game with Charlie

by John Connelly

a game

We can

play with

Handball

We can

play with

Basketball

play with

Soccer

can

play

a game

Come on! let's meet!

let's train

let's play

www.movingwell.org

Come on! let's meet!

let's train

let's play

www.movingwell.org